The Best and Worst

Caoimhe Downey

BookLeaf Publishing

India | USA | UK

Presentation by *BookLeaf Publishing*

Web: www.bookleafpub.com

E-mail: info@bookleafpub.com

ISBN: 978-93-5744-396-8

First edition 2022

PREFACE

This isn't perfect, but this is me.
Writing random and at times chaotic rhymes is my from of mental exercise. When I can't quite order the thoughts in my head, I find paper for my pen, sometimes ordered and sometimes distorted but always a true reflection. I only hope that this project can help with my progression, and that whoever finds themselves flipping through, can find comfort in what I know to be true.
Sometimes all you need is a poem or two.

I'm Dreaming

I'm dreaming of
blue skies
trees growing high
mama's and their young
the untroubled ones.

A new world
where freddos won't bankrupt
and bankers don't cheat
when kids are kids
with food to eat.

In my dream
the water's not rising
ice caps stop melting
forests aren't dying
low is carbon dioxide.

I'm dreaming of a new world.
love is love and love is free
who we are is we.

Hands
will not
wander.

Eyes
will not
stare.

Girls won't be broken
by power.
Lives not taken
by hate.

Hysteria is not
a weapon
a tool
for success.

Survivors will be outspoken
words celebrated
no longer debated.
Justice.

A world where
rich, open
their eyes
their wallets.
We open
our hearts,
minds.

Health care workers will lead
Us.

Politicians will clean
our trash.
We will fix
their mess.

Wealth won't decide health
binaries won't dictate the norm
us and them, no more.
Dreaming of a world for we
for now
for ever.

I'm dreaming of the world that could be.
A new world for you and me.
Now existing only in sleep
but full of a pure possibility.

We're Only Human

we work to live,
or live to work

we live to love,
but turn from her

we wish for wealth,
and still die poor

we fight for rights,
but turn our backs

we live in a world unsure,
struggling to stay afloat,
still we carry on
and on and on
its the best of us,
its the worst of us

we're only human,
after all.

Meant To Be.

I'm tired of seeking meaning,
when I could be living.
Making decisions based on wealth,
that fuck with my mental health.
Drowning in regrets and overthinking,
afraid my life will never begin.
We're stuck in doors that go around,
putting the lost in lost and found.
How did we get here?
Why is the future our biggest fear?
Moments are slipping away,
"what's next" is all we can say.
I need to stop and breathe,
grab life and just believe,
stop seeking who I'm meant to be,
be the living, breathing and present me.

The 'W' Word

Legend tells of a word
sparking fear when it is heard
uttered ever so softly in the herd
so as not to disturb

to claim it,
to experience censorship
burdened with pain and hatred
for simply moving your lips

there were those who wore it on their skin
proudly standing with their kin
for that they were broken
grabbed and pulled and slapped with a grin

mouths sewn shut
hair forcibly cut
clothes torn and words ignored with a 'but'
all while a fire was burning deep in the gut

bodies not trusted
feared and disgusted
by those who lusted
after which was theirs. and not for Us?

ever the imposter,
never belonging, just a bother
a nuisance, nothing more than a mother
the food maker, the dishwasher

hundreds of years as second
left to silently follow when beckoned
'stay in your place, learn your lesson'
they never expected a rebellion

fire burning deep in the gut.
rebellion rising against the 'but'.
sharpening weapons with which to cut
out of the corner, baby was put.

it starts low
but begins to grow
soon they will watch our show
and then they will know.

know the power of the word,
sparking fear when it is heard,
but no longer is it whispered,
now we scream it from our hearts.

WOMAN.
WOMAN.
WOMAN.

Here's What I Remember

I may not remember all the names, the faces,
not even the places,
how anything tasted,
the nights we were wasted.

Why we were there,
or why we were anywhere.
I'll never feel that same free air,
much to my despair.

But here's what I remember,
here is what's at the centre.

I remember
that feeling of belonging
and pure joy, pumping
through me with the beat,
happy tears, we shared
heartfelt words we whispered,
stumbling around hazy
fuelled by booze and majesty,

the long nights
while we were young.

Those are the moments I remember
the ones I hold onto.
How about you?

Jigsaw

Do you remember when we were young,
how we just knew, it had to be true, that the sun
revolved around our world day and night?
All we knew, is what was in our sight.

We couldn't be wrong.
We knew all that was going on.
Because, why must we believe
in all that we could not see?

But as we grew,
our world did too.
In fact, we were not the whole book,
just a chapter, just characters following our own
plot hook.

We were not a complete scene,
just one tiny piece
to be handled.
Around the board, we would travel.

Until we found our place
in this vast, confusing, beautiful space.
A piece of green or blue,
in the jigsaw that is our world in view.

Lessons From a Child.

In a world of leaders,
omniscient thinkers,
and teachers.
We tend to overlook,
the best voices in the book.

Those who love,
before they judge,
and believe in so much.
Those who can truly see,
the beauty in life, in you and me.

An empty box, at their age,
not empty, but their world stage,
Perhaps, a giant cage
trapping deadly beasts!
No! A train, zooming east.

A rainy day,
is never grey,
a time to be wished away,
but extra time to play and giggle,

to splash around in muddy puddles.

So many lessons we can learn from a child.
They remind us to look for joy, to embrace the
wild.
They show us the power of pure smiles
warming our hearts gone cold.
the day we did as we were told.

Everything I Never Said.

I write to you,
a list of everything I never said.
Things I knew in my heart,
that couldn't align in my head.

Things will fade,
and time will pass,
pain doesn't last forever,
is what I must say first.

Remember who you are.
Do not shapeshift to please,
or squeeze into a box, follow the crowd.
Do not dim the light for ease.

What is meant for you,
will come in time.
Don't waste your years in fear.
All will someday be fine.

Despite what they might say,

a moment on the lips,
is worth every bite.
And is never a lifetime on the hips.

Although there is more I could say,
I'll leave you with this,
All you need is you,
you have the power to grant life's wish.

Intoxicated.

Intoxicated by the buzz,
the life that surrounds,
fuels me like a drug.

All five senses attacked,
the tastes, the smells, the sounds,
the bright and warming sights that attract.

To touch an earth so rich,
in knowledge and memories,
of lives gone by, faster than an eye can twitch.

Secrets these walls do hold.
Broken hearts and lovers tiffs,
become stories forever told.

Surrounded by terracotta stones,
breathing air filled with sweetness,
while bottles of deep red clink by, to be opened
at home.

With this city, I fell in love.
My summer love affair with a smooth roast,
and all of the above.

Playing Chicken
with Your Heart

always playing chicken with your young heart
tempting fate and playing so close to fire
pounding the beating drum to see how far
your tune protects your quest of desire
a fling burning with thrill, passion and lust
touch ignites a hidden feeling inside
though doubt grows slow within, in that you
trust
play you chicken with your heart, but be wise
wise to the games, the threat to innocence
like the moon governs tides, your head leads you
as the victor will you arise from events
pull back from what is not pure nor is true
confront the pain, overcome a lost young love
from ashes rises the phoenix above

Not One But Many

not one but many
but all the same
for the foundations remain
forgotten over time
and lost inside
the small space that holds
like birds in cages of old
struggling to escape
calling out for embrace
the many faces of one
through all the pain, through all the fun
seeking who you are

but into a box you will not fit.
not one but many
and all the same
that is the magic of you

Sister

hand me downs
and daisy crowns
flipping rooms upside down
seeking treasure in lost lands
the same but different
the one to whom you vent
and bicker over rent
fires stoked by 'oh no you didn't'
but hands join as one
small shoulders leant on
secrets shared, protected from mum
best friend and greatest foe since day one

Where Do We Go?

those highest, are reaching higher
beyond the limits, behind the stars
fuelling flights by digging deeper
to the centre, our earths heart
science becomes blind to eye
and knowledge augments
the limit is no longer the sky
our priority is future tense
but how do we continue and grow
if we answer all the questions
if we know all there is to know
and learn all life's lessons
where do we go from there?

You and I

the difference between You and I
will not fade over time
nor is it something to hide
the difference between You and I
is as stark as sand and tide
just as the sun must set and the sun must rise
the difference between You and I
must forever divide
but stay with me for a while
in spite of the difference between You and I
your words will make me smile
and my heart race for miles
for now embrace the difference between You
and I
hold my hand, dream of the sky
let the only difference for now be
that You are You and I am Me

Sleep

they say sleep is for the weak
that dreams realise when awake
but I challenge you
to really be true
tell me what you dream
is all as it seems
I dream of happiness and consent
of love, choice and time well spent
but when awoken
the truth hardens
I see the pain and struggles
I see the lies and troubles
those that ensue
when we fight for dreams meant to be true

XY

because XY equals excess
would be my guess
because girls cry
while boys stand tall with pride
because blood from wounds
is cleaner than blood from wombs
a sign of great power
they can wash off in the shower
because they're stronger
but funny that we live longer?
because his voice was louder
no, because he locked her
away in the attic
and diagnosed as hysteric
just because
that's how it was
back then, in the old day
not anymore, no things have changed
lifted up and praised
we even have our own day
but still we walk often in fear
and shout just so they can hear
our demand to be safe.

Can You See Her?

Can you see her? Up there on the world's stage.
She's at the most wonderful age,
her life is bursting
with beauty, and magic, she's laughing
with glee, a kind beautiful little fool
yes, she has it all.

But I'm worried about her,
at worrying I'm an expert, a connoisseur.
I do not worry with doubts
her brightness, I'm certain about.

No, though I see the way she dazzles,
the distance her light travels.
She shines ever so bright
into the darkest of rooms she brings light.

I worry because I know how the sky
is ever so monopolised
by stars who shine as she does
they are bigger, some even brighter than little
dove.

What if her view is distorted
her light dimmed, her hope thwarted

by the abundance that is
the world in which we have to live?
How will she know to trust her voice
surrounded but so much noise?

I only hope that she will see
it is herself who controls the glee.
I only hope that she will be
All I know her to be already.

The End.

I'm figuring out my voice
seeking to calm the noise
of my head, words tumbling
tumbling and fumbling, becomes mumbling
scared to speak
not even a peep
afraid of the empty
nonsense that escapes me

I don't have much to say
or perhaps too much in a way
not 'just enough' but excess
I am but a guest
In my brain
passing through, a passenger on a train
not familiar with who I find
when I look into my mind